THE GANDHI BOOK OF QUOTES

A COLLECTION OF SPEECHES, QUOTATIONS, ESSAYS AND ADVICE

EDITED BY TRAVIS HELLSTROM

hatherleigh

Hatherleigh Press, Ltd.
62545 State Highway 10, Hobart, NY 13788, USA
hatherleighpress.com

The Gandhi Book of Quotes

Library of Congress Cataloging-in-Publication Data
is available.
ISBN: 978-1-961293-40-3

Printed in the United States
The authorized representative in the EU for product safety and compliance is Catarina Astrom, Blästorpsvägen 14, 276 35 Borrby, Sweden.
info@hatherleighpress.com

10 9 8 7 6 5 4 3 2 1

CONTENTS

INTRODUCTION

MAHĀTMĀ GANDHI's life and teachings have profoundly shaped the course of history, offering a path toward peace and justice even in the darkest of times. Born Mohandas Karamchand Gandhi in 1869 in Porbandar, India, Gandhi's journey from a young lawyer in South Africa to the leader of India's nonviolent struggle for independence is one of unparalleled courage, resilience and wisdom. He was later given the honorific title "Mahātmā" (meaning "Great Soul") by Rabindranath Tagore and others, an honor which became synonymous with his identity and which we use here in this book.

Gandhi believed that truth and nonviolence were not merely principles to be followed, but profound forces that could transform individuals, communities and nations. His emphasis on simplicity, self-discipline and service became the cornerstone of his philosophy, inspiring countless movements for civil rights and freedom across the globe. Mahātmā Gandhi's philosophy of nonviolence and truth has inspired countless leaders across the world. Martin Luther King Jr., a central figure in the American civil rights movement, directly credited Gandhi's teachings as foundational to his approach to nonviolent protest. Nelson Mandela, in his fight against apartheid in South Africa, often reflected on Gandhi's resilience and commitment to justice. The 14th Dalai Lama regularly speaks of Gandhi's influence on his beliefs in compassion and nonviolence as solutions to global challenges. Former U.S. President Barack Obama has highlighted Gandhi as a personal source of inspiration for leadership grounded in humility and service. These leaders, among many others, embody Gandhi's enduring legacy and demonstrate the global relevance of his teachings.

Here in *The Gandhi Book of Quotes*, we seek to encapsulate Gandhi's timeless wisdom by collecting his most impactful quotes. Each section delves into a specific theme central to his life's mission: truth, leadership, simplicity, social justice, education, courage, unity, spirituality, and love. These quotes are more than mere words: they are guiding principles that challenge us to reflect on our actions and strive for a better world. While many of the quotes in this collection are drawn directly from Gandhi's writings and speeches, some have been thoughtfully paraphrased from his teachings. These interpretations aim to honor the spirit of his philosophy and make his timeless wisdom more accessible to modern readers.

As you explore these pages, consider Gandhi's own reflections on the importance of personal transformation as a foundation for societal change. His message resonates now more than ever, reminding us that even the smallest acts of kindness, courage, and love can create ripples of change that extend far beyond our immediate circles. Let these quotes serve as a source of inspiration and a call to action, inviting you to embody Gandhi's vision of a compassionate and equitable world.

"My life is my message."

—MAHĀTMĀ GANDHI

Truth & Nonviolence

Mahātmā Gandhi believed that truth, or satya, *was the ultimate reality and the cornerstone of all moral action. To him, nonviolence, or ahimsa, was inseparable from the pursuit of truth. These principles guided his philosophy of life and his political strategies, emphasizing the power of love and courage over hatred and fear. Gandhi's unwavering commitment to truth and nonviolence not only liberated India from colonial rule but also inspired countless movements for justice and peace across the world.*

An error does not become truth by reason of multiplied propagation, nor does truth become error because nobody sees it.

❖ ❖ ❖

Nonviolence is the greatest force at the disposal of mankind.

❖ ❖ ❖

Truth never damages a cause that is just.

There is no god higher than truth.

Nonviolence requires more courage than violence.

Nonviolence is not a garment to be put on and off at will.

An eye for an eye will only make the whole world blind.

A man is but the product of his thoughts. What he thinks, he becomes.

⁂ ⁂ ⁂

Freedom is not worth having if it does not include the freedom to make mistakes.

⁂ ⁂ ⁂

In a gentle way, you can shake the world.

⁂ ⁂ ⁂

Prayer is not asking. It is a longing of the soul.

You must be the change you wish to see in the world.

Power based on love is
a thousand times more
effective and permanent
than the one derived from
fear of punishment.

The pursuit of truth does not permit violence on one's opponent.

The weak can never forgive. Forgiveness is the attribute of the strong.

⁂ ⁂ ⁂

Truth stands, even if there be no public support. It is self-sustained.

⁂ ⁂ ⁂

There is no way to peace; peace is the way.

⁂ ⁂ ⁂

The pursuit of truth is more important than the pursuit of success.

Nonviolence requires faith in humanity and faith in oneself.

* * *

Let us rise with courage and determination and show the world the power of truth and love.

* * *

An unjust law is itself a species of violence.

* * *

Truth and love will overcome lies and hatred.

Nonviolence begins in the heart and mind.

Prayer brings strength to the soul.

Nonviolence is not a weapon of the weak. It is a weapon of the strongest and the bravest.

There is more to life than increasing its speed.

The best politics is right action.

Faith in truth is the foundation of hope.

Nonviolence demands courage, not passivity.

To believe in something, and not to live it, is dishonest.

Anger is the enemy of nonviolence and pride is a monster that swallows it up.

The path of truth and nonviolence leads to inner peace.

Nonviolence is the antidote to chaos.

The difference between what we do
and what we are capable of doing
would suffice to solve
most of the world's problems.

Truth alone triumphs.

Leadership & Service

Gandhi saw leadership as a calling rooted in service and humility. He believed that true leaders inspire others by their actions and seek the welfare of those they serve. Service, in Gandhi's view, was the highest form of devotion, fostering a sense of unity and shared purpose.

The best way to find yourself is to lose yourself in the service of others.

⁂

Service which is rendered without joy helps neither the servant nor the served.

⁂

A life dedicated to service is a life of purpose.

True happiness is when what you think, what you say, and what you do are in harmony.

A man becomes great exactly in the degree in which he works for the welfare of his fellow-men.

No culture can live if it attempts to be exclusive.

Leadership is action, not position.

⁂ ⁂ ⁂

To lead is to inspire others to achieve their best.

⁂ ⁂ ⁂

Serve not for rewards but for the joy of serving.

⁂ ⁂ ⁂

A leader must be the first to sacrifice.

True service uplifts both the giver and the receiver.

❖ ❖ ❖

Leadership is built on the foundation of trust and respect.

❖ ❖ ❖

The highest form of leadership is leading by example.

❖ ❖ ❖

Compassion is the essence of true service.

A leader's strength is measured by their commitment to their people.

❖ ❖ ❖

Service to humanity is the path to divinity.

❖ ❖ ❖

The true leader seeks to serve, not to rule.

❖ ❖ ❖

Leadership requires courage and selflessness.

Service is the rent we pay for our place on Earth.

* * *

The greatest leader is the greatest servant.

* * *

Man becomes great when he begins to care for others.

* * *

To serve others is to serve oneself.

A life of service is a life well-lived.

Satisfaction lies in the effort, not in the attainment. Full effort is full victory.

The power of a leader lies in their ability to empower others.

Humility is the foundation of all great leadership.

A leader is not defined by their authority but by their actions.

Service is love in action.

The true measure of leadership is the impact you have on others.

A leader is a steward of the people's trust.

Great leaders build bridges, not walls.

Service is the highest expression of gratitude.

Leadership is not about being in charge; it's about taking care of those in your charge.

True leadership inspires hope and confidence in others.

❖ ❖ ❖

Gentleness, self-sacrifice, and generosity are the exclusive possession of no one race or religion.

Simplicity & Self-Discipline

Gandhi's life was a testament to the power of simplicity and self-discipline. He believed that material excess leads to spiritual emptiness, and true freedom is found by living with intention and clarity.

Live simply so that others may simply live.

Patience is not the ability to wait, but how you act while waiting.

Discipline is the bridge between goals and accomplishments.

Contentment comes from limiting one's desires.

True wealth is measured by simplicity of living.

In simplicity lies the essence of beauty.

A disciplined mind leads to true freedom.

Simplicity is a choice, not a limitation.

Happiness is not found in possessions but in contentment.

Simplicity transforms the ordinary into the extraordinary.

Self-discipline is the foundation of success.

A simple life is a peaceful life.

The art of simplicity is the art of focus.

A disciplined life is a fulfilled life.

Simplicity brings clarity to the soul.

The joy of simplicity surpasses the pursuit of luxury.

❖ ❖ ❖

True simplicity is an act of courage.

❖ ❖ ❖

A simple act can change the world.

❖ ❖ ❖

Discipline transforms intentions into actions.

❖ ❖ ❖

Mastering oneself is the greatest victory.

The greatest strength lies in simplicity.

The simple path leads to profound truth.

Simplicity nurtures the soul.

True happiness is living simply and loving deeply.

❖ ❖ ❖

Simplicity is the mother of clarity.

❖ ❖ ❖

Simplicity aligns us with nature.

❖ ❖ ❖

Simplicity and discipline pave the way to peace.

❖ ❖ ❖

The simplest things bring the greatest joy.

A life of simplicity is a life of freedom.

Simplicity is the antidote to chaos.

Discipline turns dreams into reality.

A simple life reflects a strong soul.

Simplicity clears the clutter of the mind.

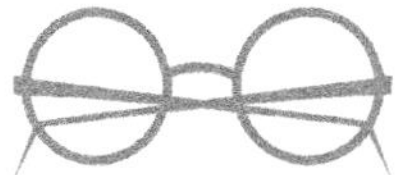

Social Justice & Equality

Gandhi's fight for equality and justice was grounded in his unwavering belief in the dignity of all people. He championed the rights of the oppressed and sought to build a society where fairness and compassion prevailed.

The true measure of any society can be found in how it treats its most vulnerable members.

⁂ ⁂ ⁂

Equality is not just a principle but a necessity for progress.

⁂ ⁂ ⁂

Justice delayed is justice denied.

⁂ ⁂ ⁂

Compassion is the foundation of equality.

No one is free until everyone is free.

True equality honors the dignity of every person.

Justice is the bond of human community.

Equality strengthens the fabric of society.

Justice inspires hope and courage.

Here is a mantra, a short one that I give you. You may imprint it on your hearts and let every breath of yours give expression to it: Do or die. We shall either free India or die in the attempt.

A just society uplifts everyone, not just a few.

Fairness is the soul of justice.

Equality is the foundation of peace.

Justice and peace go hand in hand.

Equality is the bridge to harmony.

Justice transforms individuals and societies.

A just world is a free world.

The arc of justice bends toward truth.

Equality nurtures the human spirit.

Justice strengthens the bonds of community.

The voice of justice speaks through the actions of the just.

***

True justice uplifts, not punishes.

***

Compassionate justice is lasting justice.

***

Justice without compassion is cruelty.

***

A society of equals is a society of strength.

The quest for justice begins in the heart.

Equality is the heartbeat of humanity.

The light of justice dispels the darkness of oppression.

Equality builds bridges between divides.

Justice is the foundation of a moral society.

The pursuit of equality is the pursuit of unity.

Justice brings peace to the restless soul.

Equality is the cornerstone of progress.

Education & Self-Improvement

Gandhi believed that education was not merely a tool for knowledge but a means to cultivate character, wisdom, and self-reliance. He emphasized lifelong learning and self-improvement as the path to personal and societal growth.

Live as if you were to die tomorrow. Learn as if you were to live forever.

∴ ∴ ∴

Knowledge without character is dangerous.

∴ ∴ ∴

An educated mind is a weapon in the hands of the wise.

∴ ∴ ∴

Self-improvement is the pathway to community improvement.

Wisdom grows through continuous learning.

True education is the moral development of the individual.

The aim of education is the complete development of mind and spirit.

Education is the foundation of freedom.

∴ ∴ ∴

A good education liberates the soul.

∴ ∴ ∴

A teacher affects eternity; they can never tell where their influence stops.

∴ ∴ ∴

Character is the foundation of a meaningful education.

∴ ∴ ∴

An educated person is one who learns from everyone and everything.

True learning is a journey of humility.

True knowledge is knowing oneself.

Education empowers individuals to serve humanity.

The purpose of education is to replace an empty mind with an open one.

❖ ❖ ❖

A student's duty is to learn, and a teacher's duty is to inspire.

❖ ❖ ❖

Lifelong learning is the secret to enduring wisdom.

❖ ❖ ❖

True education instills courage and integrity.

❖ ❖ ❖

The greatest learning is learning to live harmoniously.

Education is the mother of innovation.

The educated soul seeks truth and acts upon it.

Self-improvement requires discipline and determination.

A truly educated mind is never stagnant.

***

The ultimate goal of education is to serve humanity.

***

An open mind leads to endless possibilities.

***

Education begins the moment we are born and never truly ends.

***

Improvement of oneself is the improvement of the world.

Knowledge applied is wisdom.

Education and humility go hand in hand.

Education lights the path to freedom.

True education creates leaders, not followers.

***

Knowledge is power, but character is strength.

***

The pursuit of learning is the pursuit of growth.

***

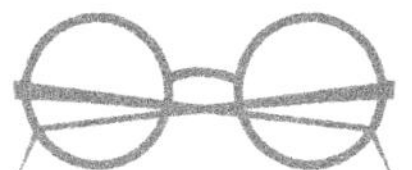

Courage & Resilience

Courage and resilience were hallmarks of Gandhi's philosophy, both in personal character and public life. He believed that bravery was not the absence of fear but the ability to act despite it, and resilience was the strength to endure challenges for a greater cause.

Strength does not come from physical capacity. It comes from an indomitable will.

⁂ ⁂ ⁂

A coward is incapable of exhibiting love; it is the prerogative of the brave.

⁂ ⁂ ⁂

You may never know what results come of your actions, but if you do nothing, there will be no result.

⁂ ⁂ ⁂

The best way to overcome fear is to face it.

Adversity is the crucible in which courage is forged.

An unflinching spirit is the backbone of progress.

Courage is not the absence of fear but the mastery of it.

In the face of despair, find strength in your purpose.

❖ ❖ ❖

Resilience is the ability to bend without breaking.

❖ ❖ ❖

Stand firm in your convictions, even if you stand alone.

❖ ❖ ❖

Courage is grace under pressure.

❖ ❖ ❖

A resilient soul turns obstacles into opportunities.

Fearlessness is the first requisite of spirituality. Cowards can never be moral.

Resilience is the quiet courage to keep going.

The storm tests the strength of the tree.

True courage is in rising after every fall.

It is easy to be brave when things go well, but true courage is revealed in adversity.

Patience and resilience are the armor of the brave.

Courage and compassion walk hand in hand.

The road to success is paved with perseverance.

A brave heart is a peaceful heart.

The strength to forgive is the strength to heal.

Resilience is the light that shines in the darkest hour.

Courage transforms weakness into strength.

In struggle, we discover our strength.

The power of resilience lies in hope.

Fear is a shadow; courage is the light that dispels it.

Resilience is the art of navigating through chaos.

⁂ ⁂ ⁂

A brave soul inspires bravery in others.

⁂ ⁂ ⁂

True courage is acting with a clear conscience.

⁂ ⁂ ⁂

Resilience is not giving up when the world pushes you down.

⁂ ⁂ ⁂

Courage is the compass that guides us through life's challenges.

❖ ❖ ❖

Adversity reveals the strength within us.

❖ ❖ ❖

A courageous heart beats with the rhythm of purpose.

❖ ❖ ❖

Unity & Community

Gandhi's vision for humanity emphasized unity and the strength of community. He believed that collaboration and understanding were the keys to overcoming divisions and building a harmonious society.

The golden way is to be friends with the world and to regard the whole human family as one.

* * *

Unity among diversity is humanity's greatest strength.

* * *

An individual is but a drop; together, we are an ocean.

* * *

A community thrives when it puts its weakest members first.

❖ ❖ ❖

Bridges are built through dialogue, not walls.

❖ ❖ ❖

The spirit of togetherness can conquer any challenge.

❖ ❖ ❖

A united people cannot be broken by fear.

❖ ❖ ❖

True community is rooted in mutual respect.

The bonds of humanity are stronger than the forces of division.

Working together, we can achieve the impossible.

Unity is not achieved by force but by understanding.

Harmony in diversity is the essence of humanity.

∴ ∴ ∴

A community of compassion creates a world of peace.

∴ ∴ ∴

Respect for others is the foundation of unity.

∴ ∴ ∴

The strength of a society is measured by the strength of its communities.

∴ ∴ ∴

Together, we can overcome any obstacle.

⁂ ⁂ ⁂

Community is the soul of humanity.

⁂ ⁂ ⁂

Unity is the bridge that connects hearts and minds.

⁂ ⁂ ⁂

The path to peace begins with unity.

⁂ ⁂ ⁂

Collaboration builds a stronger future.

A shared vision unites diverse perspectives.

True unity is born from mutual understanding.

Community is the foundation of progress.

Unity grows where kindness is sown.

A united effort brings about extraordinary change.

Unity is strength, and division is weakness.

The beauty of community lies in its diversity.

Together, we can create a better world.

The bonds of community are forged through trust.

A harmonious community fosters a peaceful society.

Unity is the light that dispels the darkness of division.

Collaboration turns dreams into reality.

Spirituality & Faith

For Gandhi, spirituality was intertwined with everyday life. His faith guided his actions and provided him with the strength to pursue justice and truth. He believed in the unity of all religions and the importance of spiritual growth.

Faith is not something to grasp; it is a state to grow into.

* * *

The essence of all religions is truth and love.

* * *

Prayer is the key of the morning and the bolt of the evening.

* * *

True spirituality is living in harmony with oneself and others.

God has no religion.

Spiritual progress is the foundation of all other progress.

The seeker of truth must be humbler than the dust.

My religion is based on truth and nonviolence.

Service to humanity is service to God.

When faith is lost, life has no meaning.

Spiritual growth begins with self-reflection.

All religions lead to the same truth.

Faith in humanity is faith in God.

Spirituality is the journey to the soul.

True prayer is a conversation with the divine.

Faith is the bridge between the seen and the unseen.

❖ ❖ ❖

Religion is a matter of the heart, not dogma.

❖ ❖ ❖

A pure heart is the temple of God.

❖ ❖ ❖

The light of faith dispels the darkness of doubt.

❖ ❖ ❖

Truth is the language of the divine.

Faith nourishes the soul.

The essence of prayer is gratitude.

Spirituality unites where division exists.

Faith gives strength to endure life's challenges.

True worship is living with integrity.

Spirituality is the art of inner peace.

Faith is the foundation of hope.

The divine resides in every heart.

Prayer connects us to the eternal.

True faith transforms the soul.

Religion is a personal journey, not a public show.

Faith is the flame that lights the way.

The spirit of truth is the spirit of God.

The path to divinity lies in service.

Love & Forgiveness

Love and forgiveness were central to Gandhi's philosophy. He believed that love had the power to heal even the deepest wounds, and forgiveness was a sign of strength, not weakness.

Love is the bridge between two worlds.

⁂

Forgiveness transforms anger into compassion.

⁂

A heart full of love knows no boundaries.

⁂

Love and forgiveness are the foundations of a peaceful life.

∴ ∴ ∴

To love deeply is to live fully.

∴ ∴ ∴

Forgiveness sets the soul free from the weight of resentment.

∴ ∴ ∴

Love is not just an emotion; it is a way of being.

∴ ∴ ∴

Forgiveness brings clarity to the heart and mind.

Where love dwells, forgiveness flourishes.

To forgive is to embrace peace over conflict.

Love illuminates even the darkest corners of the heart.

Forgiveness is the ultimate act of love.

Love knows no fear and holds no grudges.

Forgiveness opens the door to reconciliation.

Love nurtures the seeds of understanding.

To forgive is to set yourself free.

Love heals wounds that hatred deepens.

Forgiveness is a journey toward inner peace.

Love radiates beyond the barriers of hate.

Forgiveness strengthens the bonds of humanity.

A loving heart forgives without hesitation.

Love creates bridges where walls once stood.

Forgiveness is a testament to the strength of character.

To love is to recognize the divine in others.

Forgiveness renews the spirit and the soul.

Love breaks the chains of bitterness.

Forgiveness is the highest form of self-love.

Love and forgiveness are the roots of compassion.

To forgive is to choose peace over conflict.

Love sees no enemy, only humanity.

Forgiveness is the key to healing past wounds.

A life of love and forgiveness is a life of harmony.

Forgiveness restores broken relationships.

Love is the universal language of the soul.

Quotes About Gandhi

Generations to come will scarce believe that such a one as this ever in flesh and blood walked upon this earth.

—ALBERT EINSTEIN

Gandhi was inevitable. If humanity is to progress, Gandhi is inescapable. He lived, thought, and acted, inspired by the vision of humanity evolving toward a world of peace and harmony.

—MARTIN LUTHER KING JR.

The spirit of Gandhi is very much alive in India, and that spirit, I hope, will greatly influence others.

—BARACK OBAMA

Gandhi's way of life is one that marries spiritual integrity and social responsibility.

—DALAI LAMA XIV

In the darkest moments of South Africa's struggle against apartheid, we turned to Gandhi's teachings for inspiration.

—NELSON MANDELA

Gandhi's philosophy of nonviolence has impacted the moral and political thinking of humanity more than any other idea in modern history.

—JOHN F. KENNEDY

Gandhi's life reminds us that nonviolence is not passivity, but a powerful force for social transformation.

—DESMOND TUTU

He taught us that the world changes when people change themselves.

—AUNG SAN SUU KYI

If humanity is to survive, Gandhi is our teacher.

—ARNOLD TOYNBEE

Gandhi's vision can guide us in the quest for a better world.

—BAN KI-MOON

Gandhi was a man of faith, simplicity, and immense courage. He showed that the most powerful weapon is the human spirit.

—JIMMY CARTER

Mahātmā Gandhi has become an icon of peace, whose wisdom will enlighten the world forever.

—DALAI LAMA XIV

His greatness lay in his ability to translate simple ideas into revolutionary action.

—JAWAHARLAL NEHRU

The teachings of Gandhi have enriched our lives and will continue to inspire generations to come.

—INDIRA GANDHI

Gandhi's nonviolent philosophy is a universal treasure for all mankind.

—KOFI ANNAN

Ꙩ Ꙩ Ꙩ

The Mahātmā's legacy is the ultimate testimony to the power of humility and truth.

—ANTÓNIO GUTERRES

Ꙩ Ꙩ Ꙩ

I bow in reverence to Gandhi's example, a light in times of darkness.

—ANGELA MERKEL

He made us believe in the power of truth over oppression.

—VÁCLAV HAVEL

He life was his message—a simple truth with infinite power.

—WILL DURANT

Gandhi's life's work was about healing divisions and spreading love.

—ELEANOR ROOSEVELT

A Timeline of Gandhi's Life & Its Impact

The following is a timeline highlighting some of the most important moments in Mahātmā Gandhi's life and beyond:

1869: Gandhi is born on October 2 in Porbandar, Gujarat, India.

1888: Gandhi travels to London to study law at University College London.

1893: Gandhi moves to South Africa to practice law, where he experiences racial discrimination that profoundly impacts his future activism.

1906: Gandhi introduces the concept of satyagraha (nonviolent resistance) during a campaign in South Africa.

1915: Gandhi returns to India and begins his leadership in the struggle for Indian independence from British control.

1920: Gandhi becomes a leader of the Indian National Congress and launches the Non-Cooperation Movement.

1930: Gandhi leads the Salt March, a 240-mile protest against the British salt tax, marking a pivotal moment in the independence movement.

1942: Gandhi launches the Quit India Movement, demanding an end to British rule in India.

1947: India gains independence, largely due to Gandhi's efforts, though he expresses sorrow over the partition of India and Pakistan.

1948: On January 30, Gandhi is assassinated in New Delhi by Nathuram Godse, a Hindu nationalist. His legacy as the "Father of the Nation" lives on globally.

1950: The Indian Constitution, heavily inspired by Gandhi's values of equality and justice, is enacted on January 26.

1982: The film *Gandhi* wins eight Academy Awards, spreading his teachings to a global audience.

2007: The United Nations declares October 2 as the International Day of Nonviolence in honor of Gandhi.

2010: Gandhi's iconic round glasses are sold at auction, symbolizing his global cultural significance.

2019: India celebrates the 150th anniversary of Gandhi's birth, with tributes and initiatives worldwide.

Selected Speeches & Writings

GANDHI GAVE many influential speeches and wrote impactful letters that endure to this day. Here is a brief selection of these writings and speeches that encapsulate the essence of Gandhi's philosophy, offering profound insights into his unwavering commitment to truth, nonviolence, and justice.

Hind Swaraj

(1909)

Often considered Gandhi's manifesto, Hind Swaraj critiques the industrialization and materialism of modern civilization. Gandhi argues for the importance of swadeshi (self-reliance), ethical living, and the pursuit of spiritual growth over material progress. Additionally, his work provides a vision for a self-sufficient India free from British rule, achieved through nonviolence and moral regeneration. Gandhi warns against the dangers of adopting Western methods of governance and lifestyle, emphasizing that true independence must be rooted in

Indian values and traditions. The book also explores the profound connection between individual transformation and societal change, underscoring Gandhi's belief that the moral regeneration of individuals would ultimately lead to a just and harmonious society. Here are selected quotes from this work and helpful context for each.

In Hind Swaraj (1909), Gandhi doesn't just question modern civilization—he dismantles it. "This civilization is such," he writes, "that one has only to be patient and it will be self-destroyed." It promises progress but delivers emptiness. "Civilization seeks to increase bodily comforts," he says, "and it fails miserably even in doing so." What it increases instead are our wants. "Formerly, men were made slaves under physical compulsion. Now they are enslaved by temptation of money and luxuries."

Gandhi believed India wasn't conquered by British power alone. "We believe that the English have not taken India; we have given it to them." True freedom, swaraj, had nothing to do with who governed and everything to do with how we govern ourselves. "Real home-rule is self-rule or self-control," he wrote. "If we become free, India is free. And in this effort to be free ourselves, consists the real fight."

He warned them not to copy the very system that oppressed them. "The English have not taken India through sword. They have taken it through railways, telegraphs, lawyers, doctors, and education." Machines, he said, were not the problem—it was how they were used. "Machinery has begun to hold the people in bondage," Gandhi wrote. "It is necessary to realize that machinery is not necessarily our enemy, but when it masters us, it becomes so." He added, "We want the energies which God has given to us to be conserved and to be utilized by us."

Western education, too, came under sharp criticism. "To give millions a knowledge of English is to enslave them," Gandhi wrote. "It is worth noting that by receiving English education, we have enslaved the nation." He saw English as a tool for distancing Indians from their own culture and wisdom.

Even democracy didn't escape his scrutiny. "It is a superstition and ungodly thing to believe that an act of a majority binds a minority," he said, pointing to the dangers of mistaking numbers for moral truth. In contrast, Gandhi's method of resistance—satyagraha—was built on truth and sacrifice. "Passive resistance is a method of securing rights by personal suffering; it is the reverse of resistance by arms."

His vision for India wasn't about power, industry, or catching up to the West. It was about something deeper. "We want the millions of India to be happy, not to be able to say that they are happy." For Gandhi, the work of independence began within. "The only real freedom," he wrote, "is freedom from fear."

Speech at the Round Table Conference

(1931)

When Gandhi traveled to London in 1931 to attend the Second Round Table Conference, he stood before British leaders not just as a political representative, but as the moral conscience of a colonized nation. He spoke plainly, with no official title, no army behind him, and no desire for revenge. "I am here to represent the dumb, semi-starved millions of India," he said. "They do not speak English, but I speak on their behalf."

"India is not an economic dependency of Britain; she has an ancient civilization that deserves respect and freedom," he stated. And to those who suggested British rule was a civilizing force, Gandhi answered, "If a man feeds me for my degradation, I do not thank him." His presence was a challenge to the empire's moral authority. "The British people will have to wake up to the fact," he said, "that the empire, as it exists, is a negation of truth."

Gandhi believed that British rule had damaged India not only economically, but spiritually. "You have emasculated the people," he said, "you have degraded their manhood and their self-respect." He refused to play politics with India's future. "I am not pleading for mercy. I am here to ask for justice, not charity."

At the heart of his argument was a belief in nonviolence—not as a passive stance, but as an active moral force. "Nonviolence is our path," Gandhi declared, "not out of weakness, but because it is the greatest force available to humanity." He told the conference, "I do not seek to harm England. I do not seek to harm a single Englishman. I seek to convert them, not to defeat them."

He made clear that India's independence was not up for negotiation—it was inevitable. "If India wants to be free, then no power on earth can stop it," he said. "And if India does not want freedom, no power on earth can give it to her." He insisted on full swaraj, complete self-rule, not half-measures or dominion status. "You cannot make a satyagrahi accept a thing he cannot accept," Gandhi said. "He would rather die than yield dishonorably."

Despite his firm stance, Gandhi's tone remained rooted in compassion and mutual respect. "I do not wish ill to the British nation. I do not want to harm your people. I want to make friendship with you," he said. "But friendship must be on equal terms."

When pressed about the practical challenges of Indian self-rule, Gandhi replied, "If I appear to be arrogant, it is not because I feel superior. It is because I feel intensely the humiliation of my people." He didn't dress the part of a politician; he wore a simple loincloth, representing those he called "the last man." "I do not wear these clothes to show off poverty," he said. "It is the garb of my people, and I am one of them."

To the very end of the conference, Gandhi maintained that independence was not just a political goal: it was a moral imperative. "Freedom is the birthright of every nation," he said. "And as long as we do not possess it, we are in chains."

Although the conference did not yield a formal agreement, Gandhi's presence, his clarity, and his unwavering commitment to nonviolence left a lasting impact. He had traveled across the empire to speak truth to power, not in anger, but in conscience. As he once put it, "My life is my message." And in London, that message rang clear: India would be free, and it would become free by the force of truth, not violence.

The Quit India Speech

(August 8, 1942)

"Do or Die."

On the eve of the Quit India Movement, Gandhi stood before the All-India Congress Committee in Bombay and delivered one of the most defiant and stirring speeches of his life. It was a call not just for political independence but for unity, courage, and unshakable adherence to nonviolence. "I believe," he began, "that in the history of the world, there has not been a more genuinely democratic struggle for freedom than ours."

He appealed directly to the people's conscience: "Every Indian must now forget that they were ever divided into factions or castes. This is no time to quarrel amongst ourselves. We must act as one nation, one people." He knew that internal division had long been a tool of colonial control—and he would not allow it to fracture this moment.

To his countrymen, he offered a clear and powerful mantra. "Here is a mantra, a short one that I give you," he said. "You may imprint it on your hearts and let every breath of yours give expression to it: Do or die. We shall either free India or die in the attempt."

This was not a call to arms, but a call to the deepest kind of sacrifice—a spiritual and moral readiness to give everything without taking life. "Let every Indian consider himself to be a free man," Gandhi declared. "Let him behave as a free man, whether he has behind him the iron bars of a prison, or whether he is moving about freely."

He reaffirmed his commitment to ahimsa, saying, "The spirit of nonviolence can never be exhausted; it is infinite, like the universe. It must guide our every action." To those who feared that civil disobedience would bring repression, Gandhi reminded them, "A non-violent soldier of freedom will covet nothing for himself. He fights only for the freedom of his country."

He was adamant that this struggle must rise above religious and sectarian divides. "Forget the differences between Hindus and Muslims," he said. "Think of India as one indivisible whole. No power on earth can keep India enslaved if her people are united in love and nonviolence."

To the British, Gandhi spoke plainly but without hate: "I am not here to harm you. I am your friend. But I can no longer be a party to your domination over my country." He told them, "Leave India to God and if that be too much, then leave her to anarchy." It was not meant as a threat—it was a moral reckoning.

Gandhi also warned his own followers against the dangers of anger and vengeance. "Let us not degrade this movement by seeking revenge," he urged. "Violence may give us victory, but it will not give us freedom." True liberation, he believed, must come from truth and discipline. "Discipline is the essence of freedom," he said. "It is only when we have internalized our freedom that we are fit to receive it."

He made it clear that leadership was not limited to the few: "Everyone of you should from this moment onwards consider yourself a leader. No one else will lead you. You must be your own leader." Even if the Congress were banned or its leaders arrested, the movement would not die. "You may arrest me and others, but you cannot arrest the Quit India movement. It will continue to grow because it lives in the hearts of the people."

Toward the close of the speech, Gandhi's tone shifted toward hope. "India's awakening is bound to come," he said. "She will become free, and through her freedom, the world will learn the power of nonviolence." His last words were both a benediction and a challenge: "Let us rise with courage and determination and show the world the power of truth and love. Do or die."

The next day, Gandhi was arrested, along with thousands of others. But the words he spoke that night had already taken root. Across the country, from students to farmers, women to workers, millions heard the call—not with anger, but with resolve. The movement would be tested, fractured, and suppressed. But Gandhi had made it clear: "Freedom is not given—it is taken."

Letter to Lord Irwin

(March 2, 1930)

In this important letter, Gandhi explains why he plans to peacefully protest the salt tax, calling it an unjust law and part of a larger system of British oppression. Sent just days before the Salt March began, the letter became a turning point in India's fight for independence. It's one of Gandhi's clearest and most powerful statements on nonviolent resistance. What follows is the full text, dated March 2, 1930.

To His Excellency
Lord Irwin
Viceroy of India

Your Excellency,

Before embarking on the campaign of civil disobedience with which I have been for some time planning, I would fain approach you and find a way, if possible, out of the existing deadlock. I therefore crave your indulgence while I venture to intrude upon your attention a summary of the reasons that compel me to this course.

The British rule has impoverished the dumb millions by a system of progressive exploitation and by a ruinously expensive military and civil administration which the country can never afford. It has reduced us politically to serfdom. It has sapped the foundations of our culture. And, by the policy of cruel disarmament, it has degraded us spiritually. We look upon this rule as a curse. We do not want to destroy English people; we want to destroy this system. We consider it to be an iniquitous and oppressive one. It has reduced the masses of India to poverty and ignorance. We hold it to be responsible for the death of millions in famines, which are the direct result of the economic policy followed by the Government.

Your Excellency must be aware that neither you nor your predecessors have been able to deny the fact of the daily growing impoverishment of the people. I will not burden your Excellency with statistics, but it is a well-known fact that the average income of the Indian is very low, and that he is generally underfed, underclothed, and underhoused. The Government has been exploiting the masses for the benefit of a few foreign interests, and it is an established fact that the administration is the most costly in the world. This has kept the people in perpetual poverty.

The salt monopoly and the resulting taxation constitute a striking example of the iniquitous system. It has been maintained to enrich the foreign government, regardless of its harmful effects on the people. Even the poorest of the poor are denied the right to collect or make their own salt and are taxed for this necessity of life. The people are subjected to the most cruel and unjust policy. The unjust law exists, and it is our duty to remove it.

We have submitted patiently to the system and suffered for it. We have tried petitions and deputations. We have appealed to reason, but we have been met with indifference, often with contempt. We are therefore left with no option but to appeal to the highest law — that of conscience and nonviolent resistance.

We believe in no violence, physical or verbal. We do not seek to punish but to awaken.

Our goal is not to destroy the British system but to render it morally untenable. I know that it is not without a deep sense of responsibility and anguish that we have taken this decision, but we do so because we believe that no other course is left to us. We have not lost faith in British justice. But we have lost all hope that it can be secured through ordinary channels.

I respectfully say that if the British people had only listened to the voice of their own best men and women, they would have long ago recognized the justice of our cause and yielded to it. But they have not done so, and we are left to our own devices.

On bended knee, I ask you to consider our plea for justice and fairness. The salt tax represents the unjust laws we must resist. This march will demonstrate our commitment to truth and freedom.

If you persist in your policies, you leave us no choice but to resist, not out of hatred, but to awaken the humanity that we believe resides in every heart. I invite you to ponder the consequences of your policies. If you decide to repress us, we will not retaliate. We will accept suffering, but we will not cease to love you.

The movement will be launched on the 11th of March by me and a few followers from this Ashram. It is open to all those who are prepared to pay the price of suffering, to work in the cause of freedom, and to do so nonviolently.

It is, I know, open to Your Excellency to frustrate my design by arresting me. I hope that there will be tens of thousands ready to take up the work after me and in due course to lay down their lives in the same cause. The movement has nothing to hide. It is all open and above board. Its sole aim is to secure the freedom of our country by means of purest suffering.

I remain,
Your faithful servant,
M.K. Gandhi

THE FINAL FAST

(1948)

"I fast not out of despair but out of hope."

For Gandhi, a fast was not a passive act or a form of personal protest—it was a deliberate spiritual discipline, rooted in ancient Indian traditions and his own philosophy of satyagraha, or truth-force. He believed that fasting was the most powerful form of non-violent resistance when all other means had failed. It was, in his words, "a sacred thing. It is never undertaken lightly, and only after the heart has been cleansed of bitterness and the cause is just."

On January 13, 1948, Gandhi began what would be his final fast. He was 78 years old, his body frail and worn, yet his moral clarity remained unshaken. The fast lasted five days, during which he took no food and only sips of water. His aim was simple, but profound: to stop the communal violence tearing through Delhi and other parts of India in the aftermath of Partition, and to bring Hindus, Muslims, and Sikhs back from the brink of hatred and retaliation.

"I fast not out of despair," he declared on the first day, "but out of hope that love and understanding will prevail. Let us bury the hatchet of division and embrace our shared humanity."

He refused to accept that freedom could be real while hearts remained divided. "We cannot call ourselves free while our hearts remain chained by hate. Freedom is as much a matter of the spirit as of the body. I am not interested in power but in the transformation of the human heart."

In the shadow of widespread bloodshed, Gandhi called not for revenge but for reconciliation. "Hatred can be overcome only by love. Retaliation only breeds more violence." He believed that true independence would mean nothing if India became a land of fear and suspicion. "What use is independence," he asked, "if we do not learn to love our neighbor as ourselves?"

To critics who saw his fast as idealistic or even manipulative, Gandhi replied, "I do not claim to have all the answers. I only know that truth and love must guide us, or we are lost." His act of self-sacrifice was a plea to the nation's conscience. "If my death can unite Hindus and Muslims, I welcome it," he said. "I have no desire to live if the hatred between us continues."

His fast awakened a response. Leaders of different communities pledged to uphold peace, restore places of worship, and protect one another. Communal violence in Delhi began to subside. On January 18, 1948, after receiving public promises of unity and reconciliation, Gandhi ended his fast. Just ten days later, he was assassinated.

His final fast remains one of the most powerful expressions of his philosophy. "Unity cannot be forced," Gandhi said. "But it can be born through suffering and love." Even in his final days, he never abandoned his belief in the potential of humanity. "I will not submit to despair. I will cling to hope, even if I must do so alone."

In the end, Gandhi's fast was more than a protest. It was a final act of love for his country and a prayer for peace that still echoes today.

Reflections & References

As you have journeyed through the teachings and philosophies of Mahātmā Gandhi, may these quotes serve not just as words but as guiding principles to live by. Gandhi's emphasis on truth, nonviolence, simplicity, and love resonates across generations, offering timeless wisdom for a world in need of compassion and understanding. Let his words inspire your thoughts, actions, and daily interactions, as we all strive toward a more harmonious and peaceful existence.

For additional resources, writings, and insights on Mahātmā Gandhi, please visit travishellstrom.com. There, you'll find more works dedicated to Gandhi's teachings, philosophies, and enduring legacy.